Why doodle?
MY FRIENDS

Rosie Brooks

Dover Publications. Inc.
Mineola. New York

Note

There are so many things you can do with a friend: dance, go camping, share a pizza, throw snowballs, fly kites, and many other fun things. In this very special book, you'll be able to "doodle" your way to creating dozens of pictures about friends, by adding your own ideas to the ready-to-finish pages. All you need is a pencil or marker and your imagination, and you'll be doodling away before you know it!

Where are Fred and Jason's backpacks?
Draw them!

What has Justin baked for Charlotte?

How many balloons are George
and John holding?

Where are Tom and Charlotte?
Finish the picture.

Paul has brought Jane breakfast in bed.
Can you draw it?

Who are William and Ryan waving to?

Matt and David are in the candy store.
Where is the candy?

What is Luis helping Harvey carry?

What game are Cassie and Chris playing?

Show what Ken and Jamie are climbing on.

Anna and Kim are dancing to the music.
Can you draw them?

What has Vicky made Stuart for dinner?

Can you draw Max, Martin's favorite pet?

Draw matching patterns on Rosie and
Ruth's dresses.

Ian's friend Jonathan is on the swing.
Add him to the scene.

Ian's friend Joanie is on the slide.
Can you draw her?

Who is Laura talking to on the phone?
Add this friend to the picture.

What do Philip and Ed need to play tennis?
Finish the scene.

Where have Dan and Ian set up their tent?

What is Alex and Pat's new pet?

What are Oliver and Tim looking at
out of the train window?

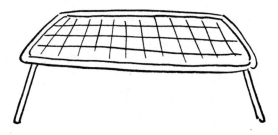

How many friends are playing on the trampoline? Show them.

Who is hiding in Luke's treehouse?

Who is watching the TV?

Show who has arrived to visit Catherine.

What toppings are Jen and Will
having on their pizzas?

Julian and Mike are on the rollercoaster.
Can you draw it?

30

How many children are in the sandbox?
Draw them.

Who is acting in the school play?

Who is riding on the back of Bill's scooter?

What can Rory and Matt see underwater?

Who is on the seesaw with Elizabeth?
Finish the picture.

How many friends are on the
deck of the ship?

To whom is Andy singing?

Can you draw the mountain that Josh and
Jim plan to ski down?

Show who is throwing snowballs
at the snowman.

Pete and Hannah are on vacation.
What is behind them? Draw it!

How many children are taking a ride
in the hot-air balloon?

What snacks have Angela and Suzy
just gotten from the food stand?

Who is David talking to through
his computer?

Finish this picture by showing
Johnny's karate partner.

Where are Steven and Josie's kites?
Show them!

Who is holding the ladder so
that Daniel can climb up?

How many birds can Ken and Jamie
see on the lake?

What have Kevin and Stan packed in their
lunchboxes? Finish the picture.

Paul and Jane are at the store. What are
they looking at in the window?

What are Fred and Jason listening
to with their headphones?

Show the decorations that Miranda and
Sue are putting up for the party.

What is growing in Tom and
Rebecca's garden?

What has Miranda brought Jen
as a get-well present?

George and Chris are in a band. Help them
play their music by drawing their guitars.

What do Catherine and Becky
need to brush their hair?

Alan and Simon are trying on hats.
Can you draw them?

Can you draw a lovely pattern on this quilt
that Charlotte and her mother are making?

Finish the painting that Al is showing
David at the museum.

Kevin and Stan would love to go in a
spaceship someday. Add them to the picture.

Where is the ball that Fred and Jason are
playing the game with?

How many friends are on the staircase?
Draw them in so they can go to the park.

Can you draw Jane's friend in the
swimming pool?

What have Luis and Harvey spotted in the
street outside?

What are Julian and Mike selling at their yard sale? Finish the picture!